Spanish Dialogues for Beginners Book 4

Book 4

Over 100 Daily Used Phrases and Short Stories to Learn Spanish in Your Car. Have Fun and Grow Your Vocabulary with Crazy Effective Language Learning Lessons

LEARN LIKE A NATIVE

www.LearnLikeNatives.com

TABLE OF CONTENT

INTRODUCTION

Before we dive into some Spanish, I want to congratulate you, whether you're just beginning, continuing, or resuming your language learning journey. Here at Learn Like a Native, we understand the determination it takes to pick up a new language and after reading this book, you'll be another step closer to achieving your language goals.

As a thank you for learning with us, we are giving you free access to our 'Speak Like a Native' eBook. It's packed full of practical advice and insider tips on how to make language learning quick, easy, and most importantly, enjoyable. Head over to LearnLikeNatives.com to access your free guide and peruse our huge selection of language learning resources.

Learning a new language is a bit like cooking—you need several different ingredients and the right technique, but the end result is sure to be delicious. We created this book of short stories for learning Spanish because language is alive. Language is about the senses—hearing, tasting the words on your tongue, and touching another culture up close. Learning a language in a classroom is a fine place to start, but it's not a complete introduction to a language.

In this book, you'll find a language come to life. These short stories are miniature immersions into the Spanish language, at a level that is perfect for beginners. This book is not a lecture on grammar. It's not an endless vocabulary list. This book is the closest you can come to a language immersion without leaving the country. In the stories within, you will see people speaking to each other, going through daily life situations, and using the most common, helpful words and phrases in language.

You are holding the key to bringing your Spanish studies to life.

Made for Beginners

We made this book with beginners in mind. You'll find that the language is simple, but not boring. Most of the book is in the present tense, so you will be able to focus on dialogues, root verbs, and understand and find patterns in subject-verb agreement.

This is not "just" a translated book. While reading novels and short stories translated into Spanish is a wonderful thing, beginners (and even novices) often run into difficulty. Literary licenses and complex sentence structure can make reading in your second language truly difficult—not to mention BORING. That's why Spanish Short

7

Stories for Beginners is the perfect book to pick up. The stories are simple, but not infantile. They were not written for children, but the language is simple so that beginners can pick it up.

The Benefits of Learning a Second Language

If you have picked up this book, it's likely that you are already aware of the many benefits of learning a second language. Besides just being fun, knowing more than one language opens up a whole new world to you. You will be able to communicate with a much larger chunk of the world. Opportunities in the workforce will open up, and maybe even your day-to-day work will be improved. Improved communication can also help you expand your business. And from a neurological perspective, learning a second language is like taking your daily vitamins and eating well, for your brain!

How To Use The Book

The chapters of this book all follow the same structure:

- A short story with several dialogs
- A summary in Spanish
- A list of important words and phrases and their English translation
- Questions to test your understanding
- Answers to check if you were right
- The English translation of the story to clear every doubt

You may use this book however is comfortable for you, but we have a few recommendations for getting the most out of the experience. Try these tips and if they work for you, you can use them on every chapter throughout the book.

1) Start by reading the story all the way through. Don't stop or get hung up on any particular words or phrases. See how much of the plot you can understand in this way. We think you'll get a lot more of it than you may expect, but it is completely normal not to understand everything in the story. You are learning a new language, and that takes time.

2) Read the summary in Spanish. See if it matches what you have understood of the plot.

3) Read the story through again, slower this time. See if you can pick up the meaning of any words or phrases you don't understand by using context clues and the information from the summary.

4) Test yourself! Try to answer the five comprehension questions that come at the end of each story. Write your answers down, and then check them against the answer key. How did you do? If you didn't get them all, no worries!

5) Look over the vocabulary list that accompanies the chapter. Are any of these the words you did not understand? Did you already know the meaning of some of them from your reading?

6) Now go through the story once more. Pay attention this time to the words and phrases you haven't understand. If you'd like, take the time to look them up to

expand your meaning of the story. Every time you read over the story, you'll understand more and more.

7) Move on to the next chapter when you are ready.

Read and Listen

The audio version is the best way to experience this book, as you will hear a native Spanish speaker tell you each story. You will become accustomed to their accent as you listen along, a huge plus for when you want to apply your new language skills in the real world.

If this has ignited your language learning passion and you are keen to find out what other resources are available, go to **LearnLikeNatives.com**, where you can access our vast range of free learning materials. Don't know where to begin? An excellent place to start is our 'Speak Like a Native' free eBook, full of practical advice and insider tips on how to make language learning quick, easy, and most importantly, enjoyable.

And remember, small steps add up to great advancements! No moment is better to begin learning than the present.

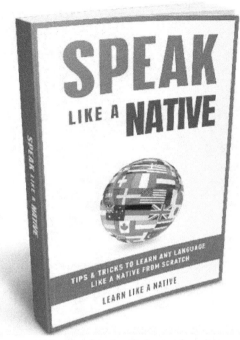

CHAPTER 1
The Driver's License / question words

HISTORIA

Wayne vive en una ciudad, tiene cuarenta años. Normalmente conduce su coche al trabajo. Wayne llega tarde al trabajo hoy, por eso conduce más y más rápido. Conduce por encima del límite de velocidad. Necesita llegar a tiempo al trabajo. Hoy tiene una reunión importante.

Wayne oye un sonido. Mira detrás de él. Hay un coche de policía detrás. Oh, no, él piensa. Voy bastante rápido. Él para el coche. El coche de policía también se detiene. Un policía sale. Camina hacia el coche de Wayne.

"Hola", dice el oficial de policía.

"Hola, señor", dice Wayne.

"**¿Por qué** crees que te detuve?", pregunta el policía.

"No lo sé. **¿Cuál** ley estoy violando?" pregunta Wayne.

"Vas muy rápido", dice el policía.

"**¿Cuántos** kilómetros por hora estoy sobre el límite de velocidad?", pregunta Wayne.

"Demasiado", dice el policía. "**¿Adónde** vas con tanta prisa?"

"A trabajar", dice Wayne.

"Muéstrame tu licencia de conducir", dice el oficial. Wayne saca su billetera. La abre. Saca su licencia de conducir. Se lo da al policía.

"Esto está caducado", dice el oficial. "Estás en grandes problemas." El oficial le dice a Wayne que no puede conducir con una licencia caducada. Debe obtener una nueva licencia. Wayne está de acuerdo. El oficial le dice que no puede conducir a trabajar hoy.

Wayne tiene que dejar de conducir su coche. Ahora debe ir a trabajar de otra forma. Él puede elegir entre el tren o el autobús. A veces, él monta su bicicleta. Si llega tarde, toma un taxi. Hoy vuelve a llegar tarde.

Wayne llega a la oficina.

"Hola, Wayne", dice su colega, Xavier. "¿**Cómo** llegaste aquí? Tu licencia está caducada, ¿verdad?"

"Sí, así es", dice Wayne. "Hoy ando en taxi. ¿**Cuán lejos** está tu casa de aquí?" Xavier suele caminar al trabajo.

"Mi casa está a un kilómetro", dice Xavier. "¿**Cuánto tarda** un taxi en llegar?"

"Unos veinte minutos", dice Wayne.

"No está mal", dice Xavier. "¿Y **cuánto** cuesta el taxi?"

"Unos veinte dólares", dice Wayne.

"Oh, eso es un poco caro", dice Xavier. "¿Qué compañía de taxis es?

"Taxi de Birmingham", dice Wayne. "¿Por qué estás tan interesado?"

"Mi familia tiene una compañía de taxis", dice Xavier. "Mi hermano la dirige."

"Bien", dice Wayne. "¿Puedo conseguir un viaje gratis?" Ambos se ríen. Wayne está bromeando. Pero necesita resolver su problema. No puede pagar un taxi todos los días. Él decide mañana que va a conseguir su licencia.

Al día siguiente, Wayne toma el autobús al Departamento de Vehículos Motorizados. Este es el edificio donde la gente obtiene su licencia de conducir. Sale de su coche. Hay una fila afuera. Mucha gente tiene que conseguir su licencia. La oficina es lenta. Él se mete en la fila. Después de una hora, está dentro del edificio. Hay otra fila. Espera.

"¿**Quién** es el siguiente?" pregunta la mujer.

"Yo", dice Wayne.

"¡Bueno, vamos!", dice. Está impaciente. "¿**Qué** necesitas?"

"Necesito renovar mi licencia", dice Wayne.

"Dame tu vieja tarjeta", dice.

"No la tengo", dice Wayne. Ella lo mira fijamente. Parece enfadada.

"¿**Por qué no** lo tienes?", pregunta.

"No la encuentro", dice Wayne.

"¿**Con quién** estoy hablando?", pregunta.

"¿Qué quieres decir?" pregunta Wayne. Está confundido.

"Vale, chico listo, dime tu nombre y apellido", dice. Wayne se lo dice.

"¿**Cuántos años** tienes?", pregunta.

"¿**Para qué**?" pregunta Wayne.

"Tengo que confirmar tu fecha de nacimiento", dice ella. "¿**Cuándo** naciste?"

Wayne le dice. Mira su computadora. Tarda mucho tiempo. Sacude la cabeza.

"No puedo encontrarte", dice. "Hay un problema con el sistema hoy. Vuelve mañana."

"No puedo", dice Wayne.

"Si quieres tu licencia hoy, tendrás que pasar el examen de conducir", dice.

"¿**Por qué**?" pregunta Wayne.

"La computadora dice que no tienes licencia", dice. Wayne necesita su licencia hoy. Él va a la otra línea. Él tomará su prueba de conducir. Fácil, piensa. Sabe conducir. Todas las demás personas son adolescentes. Él es el más viejo en esta línea.

"**¿A quién** le toca?" pregunta un hombre grande con un traje marrón.

"A mi", dice Wayne. Sigue al gran hombre hasta su coche. Se suben al coche. Wayne trata de recordar todo lo que haces en una prueba de conducción. Revisa los espejos. Se pone el cinturón de seguridad. Ve al examinador escribiendo en un bloc de notas.

"Bueno, vamos", dice el examinador.

Wayne retrocede con cuidado fuera del espacio de estacionamiento. Él conduce lentamente. Él utiliza su señal de giro. Se pone en la carretera y conduce por debajo del límite de velocidad. El examinador le dirige a través de la ciudad. Wayne se asegura de parar en las luces amarillas y utilizar su intermitente. Wayne hace un buen trabajo.

Wayne cree que pasa. El examinador lo dirige de nuevo a la oficina. Sin embargo, el examinador le dice que se detenga.

"Ahora debes aparcar en paralelo", dice el examinador. Wayne nunca aparca en paralelo. Está nervioso. El examinador le dirige a una pequeña plaza de aparcamiento. Wayne convierte el coche en el espacio. Está casi terminado de aparcar. Pero luego escucha un sonido de ding. Su coche choca con el coche detrás de él.

"Oh, no", dice Wayne.

"Eso es un fallo automático", dice el examinador. "Lo siento, no pasa la prueba de conducir."

Wayne sale del coche para dejar que el examinador conduzca el coche de vuelta a la oficina.

"**¿Cuántos** años llevas conduciendo?", pregunta el examinador.

"Veinticuatro", dice Wayne. Está avergonzado. Tiene que volver mañana.

RESUMEN

Wayne tiene una licencia de conducir. Está vencida. Wayne debe tomar taxis, autobuses y otras formas de transporte. Decide renovar su licencia. Él va a la oficina de tránsito para hacerlo. Él espera en una larga línea y tiene que responder a un montón de preguntas. Hay un problema con el sistema informático. Wayne tiene que tomar el examen de conducción de nuevo desde cero. Él hace un buen trabajo con el examinador en el coche. Sin embargo, Wayne no pasa su prueba porque no ha practicado estacionar en paralelo.

Lista de Vocabulario

why	por qué
which	cual
how many	cuántos
where	donde
how	cómo
how far	hasta dónde
how long	cuánto tiempo
how much	cuánto
who	quién
what	qué
why don't	por qué no
with whom	con quien

how old	cuántos años
what for	qué para
when	cuando
how come	cómo es que
whose	de quién
how many	cuántos

PREGUNTAS

1) ¿Por qué el oficial de policía detiene a Wayne?

    a) se pasa una luz roja

    b) su coche está roto

    c) va demasiado rápido

    d) es un criminal

2) Wayne se mete en grandes problemas con el oficial porque...

a) su licencia ha caducado

b) su coche no está registrado

c) escupe al oficial de policía

d) no responde al agente de policía

3) ¿Cuál de estos transportes cobra $20 para llevar a Wayne al trabajo?

a) bicicleta

b) autobús

c) tren

d) taxi

4) Wayne no aparece en el sistema informático de la oficina de tránsito. ¿Por qué?

a) nunca tuvo licencia

b) tiene un mal día

c) hay un problema con el sistema

d) su cumpleaños está mal

5) ¿Por qué Wayne no pasa su prueba?

a) es nuevo en la conducción

b) aparca mal porque no ha practicado este tipo de aparcamientos

c) aparca mal porque el coche es demasiado grande

d) él está borracho

RESPUESTAS

1) ¿Por qué el oficial de policía detiene a Wayne?

c) va demasiado rápido

2) Wayne se mete en grandes problemas con el oficial porque...

a) su licencia ha caducado

3) ¿Cuál de estos transportes cobra $20 para llevar a Wayne al trabajo?

d) taxi

4) Wayne no aparece en el sistema informático de la oficina de tránsito. ¿Por qué?

c) hay un problema con el sistema

5) ¿Por qué Wayne no pasa su prueba?

b) aparca mal porque no ha practicado este tipo de aparcamientos

Translation of the Story

The Driver's License

STORY

Wayne lives in a city. Wayne is forty years old. He usually drives his car to work. Wayne is late to work today. Wayne drives faster and faster. He drives over the speed limit. He needs to get to work on time. Today he has an important meeting.

Wayne hears a sound. He looks behind him. There is a police car behind him. Oh, no, he thinks. I am going rather fast. He stops the car. The police car stops, too. A policeman gets out. He walks over to Wayne's car.

"Hello," says the police officer.

"Hello, sir," says Wayne.

"**Why** do you think I pulled you over?" asks the policeman.

"I don't know. **Which** law am I breaking?" asks Wayne.

"You are going way too fast," says the policeman.

"**How many** kilometers per hour am I over the speed limit?" asks Wayne.

"Enough," says the policeman. "**Where** are you going in such a hurry?"

"To work," says Wayne.

"Show me your driver's license," says the officer. Wayne takes out his wallet. He opens it. He pulls out his driver's license. He gives it to the police officer.

"This is expired," says the officer. "You're in big trouble." The officer tells Wayne he can't drive with an expired license. Wayne must get a new license. Wayne agrees. The officer tells him he can't drive to work today. Wayne must live without a car.

Wayne has to stop driving his car. Now he goes to work other ways. He can choose between the train or the bus. Sometimes, he rides his bike. If he is late, he takes a taxi. Today, he is late again.

Wayne arrives to the office.

"Hi, Wayne," says his colleague, Xavier. "**How** did you get here? Your license is expired, right?"

"Yes, it is," says Wayne. "Today I am in taxi. **How far** is your house from here?" Xavier usually walks to work.

"My house is a kilometer away," says Xavier. "**How long** does a taxi take to get here?"

"Oh, about twenty minutes," says Wayne.

"Not bad," says Xavier. "And **how much** does the taxi cost?"

"About twenty dollars," says Wayne.

"Oh, that is a bit expensive," says Xavier. "Which taxi company is it?

"Birmingham Taxi," says Wayne. "Why are you so interested?"

"My family owns a taxi company," says Xavier. "My brother runs it."

"Nice," says Wayne. "Can I get a free ride?" They both laugh. Wayne is kidding. But he needs to solve his problem. He can't pay for a taxi every day. He decides tomorrow he is going to get his license.

The next day, Wayne takes the bus to the DMV, the Department of Motor Vehicles. This is the building where people get their driver's license. He gets out of his car. There is a line outside. Many people have to get their license. The office is slow. He gets in the line. After an hour, he is inside the building. There is another line. He waits.

"**Who** is next?" asks the woman.

"Me," says Wayne.

"Well, come on!" she says. She is impatient. "**What** do you need?"

"I need to renew my license," says Wayne.

"Give me your old card," she says.

"I don't have it," says Wayne. She stares at him. She seems angry.

"**Why don't** you have it?" she asks.

"I can't find it," says Wayne.

"**With whom** am I speaking?" she asks.

"What do you mean?" asks Wayne. He is confused.

"Ok, smart guy, tell me your first and last name," she says. Wayne tells her.

"**How old** are you?" she asks.

"**What for**?" asks Wayne.

"I have to confirm your birth date," she says. "**When** were you born?"

39

Wayne tells her. She looks at her computer. She takes a long time. She shakes her head.

"I can't find you," she says. "There is a problem with the system today. Come back tomorrow."

"I can't," says Wayne.

"If you want your license today, you will have to take the driving test over," she says.

"**How come**?" asks Wayne.

"The computer says you have no license," she says. Wayne needs his license today. He goes to the other line. He will take his driver's test. Easy, he thinks. He knows how to drive. All the other people are teenagers. He is the oldest in this line.

"**Whose** turn is it?" asks a big man with a brown suit.

"Mine," says Wayne. He follows the big man to his car. They get in the car. Wayne tries to remember everything you do in a driver's test. He checks the mirrors. He puts on his seatbelt. He sees the examiner writing on a notepad.

"Okay, let's go," says the examiner.

Wayne carefully backs out of the parking space. He drives slowly. He uses his turn signal. He gets on the road and drives under the speed limit. The examiner directs him through the town. Wayne makes sure to stop at yellow lights and to use his blinker. Wayne does a good job.

Wayne thinks he passes. The examiner directs him back to the DMV. However, the examiner tells him to stop.

"Now you must parallel park," says the examiner. Wayne never parallel parks. He is nervous. The examiner directs him to a tiny parking space. Wayne turns the car into the space. He is almost finished parking. But then he hears a 'ding' sound. His car hits the car behind him.

"Oh, no," says Wayne.

"That is an automatic fail," says the examiner. "Sorry, you fail your driver's test."

Wayne gets out of the car to let the examiner drive the car back to the office.

"How many years have you been driving?" asks the examiner.

"Twenty-four," says Wayne. He is ashamed. He has to come back tomorrow.

CHAPTER 2
At the Travel Agency / likes and dislikes

HISTORIA

Yolanda y Zelda son hermanas. Tienen vidas muy ocupadas. Ambas viven en la ciudad de Nueva York. Yolanda es peluquera para celebridades. Zelda es abogada y tiene dos hijos. Están muy ocupadas, a veces no se ven durante meses.

Yolanda tiene una idea un día. Llama a Zelda.

"¡Zelda, querida! ¿Cómo estás?", pregunta.

"Bien, hermana", dice Zelda. "¿Cómo estás?"

"¡Genial! He tenido una idea maravillosa", dice Yolanda. "¡**Deberíamos** hacer un viaje juntas!"

"Qué gran idea", dice Zelda. "¡**Me encanta**! ¿A dónde?"

"No sé, donde sea", dice Yolanda. "¡Donde sea! **¡Me encantaría** ir contigo a cualquier parte!"

"Vayamos a la agencia de viajes mañana", dice Zelda. "Ellos nos pueden ayudar."

Las hermanas se encuentran al día siguiente. Zelda trae páginas de investigación sobre vacaciones. Las páginas hablan de diferentes tipos de turismo. Hay turismo recreativo, como relajarse y divertirse en la playa. Hay turismo cultural como visitas turísticas o museos para aprender sobre historia y arte. El turismo de aventura es para personas que **adoran** explorar lugares distantes y actividades extremas. El ecoturismo es viajar a ambientes naturales.

Yolanda lee los periódicos. Turismo saludable es viajar para cuidar tu cuerpo y mente visitando lugares como balnearios. El turismo religioso es un viaje para celebrar eventos religiosos o visitar lugares religiosos importantes.

"Hay muchos tipos de viajes", dice Yolanda.

"Sí", dice Zelda. "**Me gusta** viajar por una razón. No soporto estar acostada en la playa, sin hacer nada." A Yolanda le gusta la playa. Le gusta no hacer nada de vacaciones. No dice nada.

Las hermanas llegan a la agencia de viajes. La agente de viajes es una mujer. Ella parece agradable. Yolanda y Zelda se sientan con ella.

"¿Cómo puedo ayudarte?", pregunta la agente.

"Nos gustaría hacer un viaje", dice Yolanda.

"¿Qué clase de viaje?" pregunta la agente.

"**Me enloquece** la cultura", dice Zelda. "Me encantan los museos. Me encanta el arte."

"**Prefiero** ir a algún lugar con sol. Me encantan las actividades al aire libre", dice Yolanda.

"La gente viaja por muchas razones", dice la agente. "¿Qué tal Barcelona?"

"No lo sé", dice Zelda. "**No soporto** no saber el idioma local."

"No hablamos español", dice Yolanda.

"¿Te gustaría París?", pregunta la agente. "Hay muy buenos museos y restaurantes."

"¡Nosotras tampoco hablamos francés!", dicen ambas.

"¿Qué tal Londres?", pregunta el agente.

"¡Genial!", dice Zelda.

"¡Tan lluvioso!" dice Yolanda al mismo tiempo. Las hermanas se miran.

"¡Dijiste que no te importaba Yoli!", dice Zelda.

"Quiero viajar contigo", dice Yolanda. "Pero **no me molesta** Londres. ¡**Detesto** la lluvia!"

"Vamos, Yolanda", dice Zelda. "¡Por favor!"

La agente muestra las fotos de las mujeres de Londres. Ven los edificios famosos. Yolanda le gustaría ver el Big Ben. Zelda está entusiasmada con el museo de arte moderno Tate.

"¿Qué tipo de hotel le gustaría?", pregunta la agente.

"Podríamos conseguir un apartamento en Airbnb", dice Yolanda.

"No, **detesto** quedarme en casas ajenas", dice Zelda.

"Tenemos hermosos hoteles en el centro de la ciudad", dice el agente.

"Eso suena genial", dice Zelda.

Zelda prefiere los hoteles de lujo. Sabe que a Yolanda **no le gustan mucho** los hoteles de lujo. Pero Zelda nunca se va de vacaciones. Ella quiere que estas vacaciones sean perfectas. La agencia de viajes muestra las fotos a las hermanas. Las habitaciones del hotel son enormes. Algunos tienen un baño en el medio de la habitación.

"Son magníficos", dice Zelda. "¿Te importa si nos quedamos en un hotel de lujo, Yolanda?"

"**Para nada**", dice Yolanda. Zelda sabe que **no le gustan** los hoteles de lujo. Yolanda se siente triste. Zelda hace lo que quiere.

"**¿Qué les gustaría** hacer en Londres?", pregunta la agente de viajes.

"Nos encantaría ir a todos los museos, visitar el Palacio y algunas galerías de arte", dice Zelda.

"Está bien", dice la agente de viajes. "Eso es probablemente suficiente para llenar su tiempo en Londres."

Yolanda no dice nada. Las hermanas pagan y dejan la agencia de viajes. Zelda está contenta. Yolanda desea que las vacaciones sean más de su estilo. Se va a casa. Piensa en el viaje. Sonríe. Tiene un plan.

Al día siguiente, Yolanda vuelve a la agencia de viajes.

"Hola, Yolanda", dice la agente. "¿Cómo puedo ayudarte?"

"**Queremos** cambiar un poco nuestro viaje", dice Yolanda.

"No hay problema", dice el agente de viajes.

"**Preferiríamos** ir a algún lugar soleado", dice Yolanda.

"Por supuesto", dice la agente de viajes. La agente de viajes sugiere muchos lugares diferentes. Yolanda firma algunos papeles nuevos. Le da dinero a la agente por el cambio. Se imagina a

Zelda de vacaciones. Sonríe. A Zelda **le gustan** las sorpresas.

Es fin de semana. Es hora del viaje de Yolanda y Zelda. Las hermanas se encuentran en el aeropuerto. Están emocionadas. Yolanda está nerviosa.

"Te traje café", dice. Zelda toma el café.

"Gracias", dice. Toma un sorbo. "¡Oh, pero **odio** el azúcar en mi café, Yoli!"

Yolanda se disculpa. Toma los dos cafés en sus manos. Ahora no puede llevar su maleta.

Las dos hermanas pasan por seguridad. Esperan para abordar el avión. La pantalla dice "Vuelo 361

a Londres / Con conexiones / British Airways".
Yolanda sonríe al subir al avión.

El vuelo dura seis horas. Yolanda y Zelda duermen. Se despiertan cuando el avión llega al aeropuerto de Londres. La azafata utiliza el altavoz. "Si se aloja en Londres o tiene una conexión, por favor póngase de pie y deje el avión."

Zelda se levanta. Yolanda no.

"Vamos, Yolanda", dice Zelda.   Yolanda no se mueve.

"¡Vamos!", dice Zelda.

"En realidad, hermana", dice Yolanda. "Hay un cambio de planes. Nos quedaremos en este avión."

Zelda parece estar confundida.

La azafata utiliza el altavoz de nuevo. "Si usted está viajando a nuestro próximo destino, permanezca en sus asientos. ¡Próxima parada-Fiji!"

RESUMEN

Dos hermanas, Yolanda y Zelda, quieren hacer un viaje juntas. Van a la agencia de viajes. Son muy diferentes. Es difícil para ellas acordar un lugar. A Zelda le gusta planear vacaciones y ver arte y cultura. Finalmente, deciden a dónde quieren ir. Pero al día siguiente, Yolanda vuelve a la agencia de viajes. Cambia de destino. Zelda se entera cuando su avión aterriza.

Lista de Vocabulario

we should	deberíamos

I love	Me encanta
I would love	Me encantaría
I adore	Yo adoro
I enjoy	Disfruto
I can't stand	No puedo estar de pie
we would like	nos gustaría
I'm crazy about	Estoy loco por
I prefer	Prefiero
I can't bear	No lo puedo soportar
would you like	te gustaría
I'm not mad about	No estoy enojado por
I detest	Detesto
I loathe	Odio
doesn't like	no le gusta
very much	mucho
not at all	para nada

dislikes	disgustos
what would you like	¿qué te gustaría
we want	queremos
we would rather	preferiríamos
likes	gustar
I hate	Yo odio

PREGUNTAS

1) ¿Cómo se conocen Yolanda y Zelda?

    a) son amigas

    b) son hermanas

    c) trabajan juntas

    d) son vecinas

2) ¿Qué le gusta hacer a Zelda de vacaciones?

a) ver arte y cultura

b) tumbarse en la playa

c) relajarse

d) ver lo que sucede sin planes

3) ¿Cuál de las siguientes decisiones hace Yolanda en la primera reunión con la agencia de viajes?

a) a dónde ir

b) Lugar de estancia

c) qué hacer

d) ninguna de las anteriores

4) ¿Qué hace Yolanda cuando va a la agencia de viajes por segunda vez?

a) pide su dinero de vuelta

b) cancela el viaje

c) cambia el destino

d) llama a Zelda

5) ¿Qué sucede cuando las hermanas aterrizan en Londres?

a) van a su hotel

b) van a un museo

c) el avión se estrella

d) Yolanda sorprende a Zelda con un nuevo destino

RESPUESTAS

1) ¿Cómo se conocen Yolanda y Zelda?

b) son hermanas

2) ¿Qué le gusta hacer a Zelda de vacaciones?

a) ver arte y cultura

3) ¿Cuál de las siguientes decisiones hace Yolanda en la primera reunión con la agencia de viajes?

    d) ninguna de las anteriores

4) ¿Qué hace Yolanda cuando va a la agencia de viajes por segunda vez?

    c) cambia el destino

5) ¿Qué sucede cuando las hermanas aterrizan en Londres?

    d) Yolanda sorprende a Zelda con un nuevo destino

Translation of the Story

At the Travel Agency

STORY

Yolanda and Zelda are sisters. They have very busy lives. They both live in New York City. Yolanda is a hairdresser for celebrities. Zelda is a lawyer and has two children. They are so busy, sometimes they don't see each other for months.

Yolanda has an idea one day. She calls Zelda.

"Zelda, dear! How are you?" she asks.

"Fine, sis," says Zelda. "How are you?"

"Great! I've had a marvelous idea," says Yolanda. "**We should** take a trip together!"

"What a great idea," says Zelda. "**I love** it! Where to?"

"I don't know, anywhere," says Yolanda. "Wherever! **I would love** to go anywhere with you!"

"Let's go to the travel agency tomorrow," says Zelda. "They can help."

The sisters meet the next day. Zelda brings pages of research on vacations. The pages talk about different types of tourism. There is recreational tourism, like relaxing and having fun at the beach. There's cultural tourism like sightseeing or visiting museums to learn about history and art.

Adventure tourism is for people who **adore** exploring distant places and extreme activities. Ecotourism is traveling to natural environments.

Yolanda reads the papers. Health tourism is travel to look after your body and mind by visiting places like spa resorts. Religious tourism is travel to celebrate religious events or visit important religious places.

"There are so many types of travel," says Yolanda.

"Yes," says Zelda. "**I enjoy** traveling for a reason. I can't stand lying on the beach, doing nothing." Yolanda likes the beach. She likes doing nothing on vacation. She doesn't say anything.

The sisters arrive to the travel agency. The travel agent is a woman. She seems nice. Yolanda and Zelda sit down with her.

"How can I help you?" asks the agent.

"We would like to take a trip," says Yolanda.

"What kind of trip?" asks the agent.

"**I'm crazy about** culture," says Zelda. "I love museums. I love art."

"**I would rather** go somewhere with sunshine. I love outdoor activities," says Yolanda.

"People travel for lots of reasons," says the agent. "How about Barcelona?"

"Oh, I don't know," says Zelda. "**I can't bear** not knowing the local language."

"We don't speak Spanish," says Yolanda.

"Would you like Paris?" asks the agent. "There are very good museums and restaurants."

"We don't speak French, either!" they both say.

"How about London?" asks the agent.

"Great!" says Zelda.

"So rainy!" says Yolanda at the same time. The sisters look at each other.

"You said you don't care Yoli!" says Zelda.

"I want to travel with you," says Yolanda. "**I'm not mad about** London, though. **I detest** the rain!"

"Come on, Yolanda," says Zelda. "Please!"

The agent shows the women pictures of London. They see the famous buildings. Yolanda would like to see Big Ben. Zelda is excited about the Tate Modern art museum.

"What kind of hotel would you like?" asks the agent.

"We could get an Airbnb apartment," says Yolanda.

"No, **I loathe** staying in other people's homes," says Zelda.

"We have beautiful hotels in the center of the city," says the agent.

"That sounds great," says Zelda.

Zelda prefers luxurious hotels. She knows Yolanda **doesn't like** fancy hotels **very much**. But Zelda never goes on vacation. She wants this vacation to be perfect. The travel agent shows the sisters pictures. The hotel rooms are huge. Some have a bath in the middle of the room.

"Those are gorgeous," says Zelda. "Do you mind if we stay in a fancy hotel, Yolanda?"

"**Not at all**," says Yolanda. Zelda knows she **dislikes** fancy hotels. Yolanda feels sad. Zelda does what she wants.

"**What would you like** to do while in London?" asks the travel agent.

"We would love to go to all the museums, visit the Palace, and visit some art galleries," says Zelda.

"Okay," says the travel agent. "That's probably enough to fill your time in London."

Yolanda doesn't say anything. The sisters pay and leave the travel agent. Zelda is happy. Yolanda wishes the vacation was more her style. She goes home. She thinks about the trip. She smiles. She has a plan.

The next day, Yolanda returns to the travel agent.

"Oh hello, Yolanda," says the agent. "How can I help you?"

"**We want** to change our trip a bit," says Yolanda.

"No problem," says the travel agent.

"**We would rather** go to somewhere sunny," says Yolanda.

"Of course," says the travel agent. The travel agent suggests many different locations. Yolanda signs some new papers. She gives the agent money for the change. She imagines Zelda on vacation. She smiles. Zelda **likes** surprises.

It is the weekend. It is time for Yolanda and Zelda's trip. The sisters meet at the airport. They are excited. Yolanda is nervous.

"I brought you coffee," she says. Zelda takes the coffee.

"Thanks," she says. She takes a sip. "Oh, but **I hate** sugar in my coffee, Yoli!"

Yolanda apologizes. She takes both coffees in her hands. Now she can't carry her suitcase.

The two sisters go through security. They wait to board the plane. The screen says "Flight 361 to London / With Connections / British Airways". Yolanda smiles as they get on the plane.

The flight lasts six hours. Yolanda and Zelda sleep. They awake as the plane pulls into the airport in London. The flight attendant uses the speaker. "If you are staying in London or have a connection, please stand and leave the plane."

Zelda stands up. Yolanda does not.

"Come on, Yolanda," says Zelda. Yolanda doesn't move.

"Let's go!" says Zelda.

"Actually, sis," says Yolanda. "There is a change of plans. We are staying on this plane."

Zelda looks confused.

The flight attendant uses the speaker again. "If you are traveling through to our next destination, remain in your seats. Next stop—Fiji!"

CHAPTER 3
Valentine's Day in Paris / prepositions

HISTORIA

Charles y Dana son novio y novia. Están enamorados. Charles quiere hacer algo especial para el Día de San Valentín. Invita a Dana a París. París se llama la ciudad del amor. Mucha gente viaja a París para pasar tiempo romántico con su pareja. ¿Tal vez son las películas, la comida, los hermosos edificios? París siempre se siente romántico.

La pareja llega a París el 13 de febrero. El avión aterriza. Están encantados. Charles y Dana recogen su equipaje.

"Vamos al hotel", dice Charles.

"¿Cómo?", pregunta Dana.

"Podemos tomar el tren al centro de la ciudad", dice Charles. **Delante** de la pareja hay una señal para el tren del aeropuerto. Siguen las flechas, caminando **por debajo** de ellas. Caminan **a través** del puente del cielo, hasta que llegan a la entrada del tren. Ellos van a la máquina de boletos.

"¿Qué boleto compramos?" pregunta Dana. Ambos miran fijamente la máquina.

"No lo sé", dice Charles. "El hotel está **en** el 7mo distrito." Charles adivina qué boleto comprar. Él lo compra y van a la plataforma del tren. Por

encima de las vías, hay una señal. Dice a dónde va cada tren. Un tren se acerca. El letrero dice "Centre-ville". Se suben al tren.

Cuando el tren llega al destino, se **bajan** del tren. Suben las escaleras del metro. Salen al exterior. La Torre Eiffel está **sobre** ellos.

"Es hermoso", dice Dana.

"Sí, es increíble", dice Charles.

"Quiero llegar **a la cima**", dice Dana.

"¿Sabías que pintan la torre cada siete años?" pregunta Charles. "¡Con 50 toneladas de pintura!"

"No lo sabía", dice Dana. Charles le cuenta más sobre la Torre Eiffel. Fue construida en 1889. Lleva el nombre de Gustave Eiffel, el arquitecto a cargo del proyecto. Durante 41 años, fue la estructura más alta del mundo. Hay muchas réplicas de la torre **alrededor** del mundo. Incluso hay una réplica de tamaño completo en Tokio.

"Me encanta París", dice Dana.

"Vamos al hotel", dice Charles. Caminan hasta el hotel cercano. Está justo **detrás** de la Torre Eiffel.

El día siguiente es San Valentín. La pareja tiene un almuerzo especial planeado. Van al restaurante Epicure. Es uno de los restaurantes más románticos de la ciudad.

"¿Estás lista?", pregunta Charles.

"Sí", dice Dana. "¿Cómo llegamos allí?" Salen **fuera** del hotel.

"Está **pasando** los Campos Elíseos", dice Charles. Caminan **por** la calle. Caminan **hacia** el río. Es un día hermoso. El sol brilla. Dana nota lo hermosos que son los edificios. Todos son muy antiguos.

"Deberíamos tener edificios como este en América", dice Dana.

"Son más viejos que América", dice Charles. Charles y Dana caminan **a lo largo** del río. Se toman de la mano. París es una ciudad para los amantes.

Epicure está **cerca** del distrito comercial central. Pasan por tiendas como Louis Vuitton y Pierre

Hermé. Dana se detiene a mirar por las ventanas. El restaurante está **al lado** de una de sus tiendas favoritas.

"Por favor, podemos entrar", dice ella. Cuando **pasan por** la puerta de Hermes, Carlos sabe que está en problemas. Bolsos y bufandas hay en todas partes. Dana se vuelve loca. Ella toma dos bufandas de una exhibición. Agarra un bolso de **entre** una pila de bolsos.

"¿Por favor, Charles?", le pregunta. "¿Un pequeño recuerdo de París?" piensa Charles. Los tres artículos cuestan lo mismo que el billete de avión a París. Es el día de San Valentín, sin embargo. Él dice que sí. Dana lleva las bufandas y el bolso a la caja registradora. Charles paga con su tarjeta de crédito.   Salen de la tienda. Dana está muy contenta.

Charles y Dana siguen por la calle. No ven Epicure.

"Está justo aquí", dice Charles.

"¿Justo dónde?" pregunta Dana.

"Aquí", dice Charles. "Eso es lo que dice Google Maps."

"No lo veo", dice Dana.

Charles llama al restaurante con su celular. "Hola, no podemos encontrar el restaurante", dice. Escucha. La persona habla francés. "¿Hablas inglés? ¿No?" La persona cuelga.

"No hablan inglés", dice Charles.

"Tiene que estar aquí", dice Dana. Ve un pequeño callejón. Entra en el callejón y camina un poco.

"Aquí está", dice. El restaurante está **dentro** del callejón, escondido **al final**.

"Gracias a Dios", dice Charles. "¡Ya llegamos tarde!" Entran en el restaurante.

"¿Tiene una reserva?", pregunta el camarero.

"Sí", dice Charles. "Llegamos un poco tarde. Charles."

"Síganme", dice el camarero. Siguen al camarero. Caminan entre mesas con manteles blancos. Son los primeros comensales. El restaurante está vacío.

"Es hermoso", dice Dana. Se sientan en su mesa. Tiene flores frescas en ella. Su mesa está al lado del fuego. Un candelabro de oro cuelga del techo.

"¿Qué les gustaría?", pregunta el camarero.

"El pollo con setas, y los macarrones con foie gras y alcachofa", dice Charles.

"Recomiendo los macarrones **antes** del pollo", dice el camarero.

"Está bien", dice Charles.

"El pollo se sirve con una ensalada", dice el camarero.

"Perfecto", dice Charles. "Y por favor tráenos un poco de champaña." Charles guiña un ojo al camarero.

"¿Por qué le guiñaste el ojo?", pregunta Dana.

"¡No fue mi intención!", dice Charles.

Dana y Charles están muy contentos. El restaurante es uno de los mejores de París. Tiene tres estrellas Michelin. El camarero viene **detrás** de Charles con los macarrones. Es muy rico. Tiene trufa negra en la parte superior. Están de acuerdo, son los mejores macarrones que han tenido.

El camarero lleva un carro a la mesa. Tiene dos copas, una botella de champán y una caja negra. El camarero abre el vino y lo sirve para Charles y Dana. Deja la caja negra sobre la mesa.

"¿Qué es eso?" pregunta Dana.

"Dana, ¿te casarás conmigo?" pregunta Charles. Levanta la parte superior de la caja negra. **Debajo** hay un enorme anillo de diamantes. Lo pone en el dedo de Dana.

"¡Sí!" grita Dana.

París es la ciudad del amor.

RESUMEN

Charles y Dana están enamorados. Hacen un viaje a París para el Día de San Valentín. Se pierden buscando su hotel. No entienden el metro. Ni Charles ni Dana hablan francés. Charles reserva un almuerzo especial para el Día de San Valentín. Dana no puede resistir las tiendas de París. Tienen dificultades para encontrar el restaurante. Dana encuentra el restaurante en un callejón. En el almuerzo, Charles tiene una sorpresa secreta para Dana. ¿Qué es? Una muestra de amor verdadero. Un camarero en el restaurante trae el anillo con el champán. Charles le pide a Dana que se case con él.

Lista de Vocabulario

in front of	delante de
beneath	debajo
across	a través de

in	en
above	encima de
into	en
off	fuera
above	más arriba
to	a
around	alrededor
behind	detrás
out of	fuera de
past	pasado
down	abajo
toward	hacia
along	a lo largo
near	cerca
next to	al lado de
through	a través

from	desde
amongst	entre
within	dentro de
at	en
between	entre
on	en
beside	al lado
before	antes de
with	con
behind	detrás
below	debajo

PREGUNTAS

1) ¿Quién tuvo la idea de ir de vacaciones a París?

   a) Charles

b) el padre de Charles

c) la agencia de viajes

d) Dana

2) ¿Qué es lo primero que Charles y Dana ven en París?

a) el Louvre

b) los Campos Elíseos

c) el hotel

d) la Torre Eiffel

3) ¿Qué otra ciudad del mundo tiene una Torre Eiffel de tamaño completo?

a) Nueva York

b) Tokio

c) Dubái

d) Hong Kong

4) ¿Qué convence Dana a Charles de hacer el Día de San Valentín?

    a) ir a casa

    b) ir al museo

    c) comprarle algo en Hermes

    d) dejar de beber

5) ¿Cómo le da Charles a Dana el anillo de compromiso?

    a) un camarero lo saca con el champán

    b) lo pone en su helado

    c) lo toma de su bolsillo

    d) se pone de rodillas

RESPUESTAS

1) ¿Quién tuvo la idea de ir de vacaciones a París?

a) Charles

2) ¿Qué es lo primero que Charles y Dana ven en París?

d) la Torre Eiffel

3) ¿Qué otra ciudad del mundo tiene una Torre Eiffel de tamaño completo?

b) Tokio

4) ¿Qué convence Dana a Charles de hacer el Día de San Valentín?

c) comprarle algo en Hermes

5) ¿Cómo le da Charles a Dana el anillo de compromiso?

a) un camarero lo saca con el champán

Translation of the Story

Valentine's Day in Paris

STORY

Charles and Dana are boyfriend and girlfriend. They are in love. Charles wants to do something special for Valentine's Day. He invites Dana to Paris. Paris is called the city of love. Many people travel to Paris to spend romantic time with their partner. Maybe it is the movies, the food, the beautiful buildings? Paris always feels romantic.

The couple arrives to Paris on February 13. The plane lands. They are thrilled. Charles and Dana collect their baggage.

"Let's go to the hotel," says Charles.

"How?" asks Dana.

"We can take the train to the city center," says Charles. **In front of** the couple is a sign for the airport train. They follow the arrows, walking **beneath** them. They walk **across** the sky bridge, until they come to the entrance to the train. They go up to the ticket machine.

"Which ticket do we buy?" asks Dana. They both stare at the machine.

"I don't know," says Charles. "The hotel is **in** the 7th arrondissement." Charles guesses which ticket to buy. He buys it and they go to the train platform. **Above** the tracks, there is a sign. It tells where each train is going. A train approaches. The sign says 'centre-ville'. They get **into** the train.

When the train reaches the destination, they get **off** the train. They go up the metro stairs. They step outside. The Eiffel Tower stands **above** them.

"It's beautiful," says Dana.

"Yes, it's amazing," says Charles.

"I want to go **to** the top," says Dana.

"Did you know they paint the tower every seven years?" asks Charles. "With 50 tons of paint!"

"I didn't know that," says Dana. Charles tells her more about the Eiffel Tower. It was built in 1889. It is named after Gustave Eiffel, the architect in charge of the project. For 41 years, it was the tallest structure in the world. There are many replicas of the tower **around** the world. There is even a full-size replica in Tokyo.

"I love Paris," says Dana.

"Let's go to the hotel," says Charles. They walk to the nearby hotel. It is just **behind** the Eiffel Tower.

The next day is Valentine's Day. The couple has a special lunch planned. They go to the restaurant Epicure. It is one of the city's most romantic restaurants.

"Are you ready?" asks Charles.

"Yes," says Dana. "How do we get there?" They walk **out of** the hotel.

"It is just **past** the Champs-Élysées," says Charles. They walk **down** the street. They walk **toward** the river. It is a beautiful day. The sun is shining. Dana notices how beautiful the buildings are. They are all very old.

"We should have buildings like this in America," says Dana.

"They are older than America," says Charles. Charles and Dana walk **along** the river. They hold hands. Paris is a city for lovers.

Epicure is **near** the central shopping district. They pass shops like Louis Vuitton and Pierre Hermé. Dana stops to look in the windows. The restaurant is **next to** one of her favorite shops.

"Please can we go in," she says. When they go **through** the door of Hermes, Charles knows he is in trouble. Purses and scarves are everywhere. Dana goes crazy. She takes two scarves **from** a display. She grabs a bag from **amongst** a pile of purses.

"Please, Charles?" she asks him. "A little Paris souvenir?" Charles thinks. The three items cost the same as the airplane ticket to Paris. It is Valentine's Day, though. He says yes. Dana takes the scarves and the purse to the cash register. Charles pays with his credit card. They leave the shop. Dana is very content.

Charles and Dana continue down the street. They don't see Epicure.

"It is right here," says Charles.

"Right where?" asks Dana.

"Here," says Charles. "That is what Google maps says."

"I don't see it," says Dana.

Charles calls the restaurant on his cell phone. "Hello, we cannot find the restaurant," he says. He listens. The person speaks French. "Do you speak English? No?" The person hangs up.

"They don't speak English," says Charles.

"It has to be here," says Dana. She spots a small alley. She enters the alleyway and walks a bit.

"Here it is," she says. The restaurant is **within** the alleyway, hidden **at** the very end.

"Thank goodness," says Charles. "We are already late!" They enter the restaurant.

"Do you have a reservation?" asks the waiter.

"Yes," says Charles. "We are a bit late. Charles."

"Follow me," says the waiter. They follow the waiter. They walk between tables with white tablecloths. They are the first diners. The restaurant is empty.

"It's beautiful," says Dana. They sit at their table. It has fresh flowers **on** it. Their table is **beside** the fire. A golden chandelier hangs from the ceiling.

"What would you like?" asks the waiter.

"The chicken with mushrooms, and the macaroni with foie gras and artichoke," says Charles.

"I recommend the macaroni **before** the chicken," says the waiter.

"Ok," says Charles.

"The chicken is served with a side salad," says the waiter.

"Perfect," says Charles. "And please bring us some champagne." Charles winks at the waiter.

"Why did you wink at him?" asks Dana.

"I didn't mean to!" says Charles.

Dana and Charles are very happy. The restaurant is one of the best in Paris. It has three Michelin stars. The waiter comes up **behind** Charles with the macaroni. It is very rich. It has black truffle on top. They agree, it is the best macaroni they have ever had.

The waiter rolls a cart to the table. It has two glasses, a bottle of champagne, and a black box. The waiter opens the wine and pours it for Charles and Dana. He leaves the black box on the table.

"What's that?" asks Dana.

"Dana, will you marry me?" asks Charles. He lifts the top of the black box. **Below** is a huge diamond ring. He puts it on Dana's finger.

"Yes!" shouts Dana.

Paris really is the city of love.

CONCLUSION

You did it!

You finished a whole book in a brand new language. That in and of itself is quite the accomplishment, isn't it?

Congratulate yourself on time well spent and a job well done. Now that you've finished the book, you have familiarized yourself with over 500 new vocabulary words, comprehended the heart of 3 short stories, and listened to loads of dialogue unfold, all without going anywhere!

Charlemagne said "To have another language is to possess a second soul." After immersing yourself in this book, you are broadening your horizons and opening a whole new path for yourself.

Have you thought about how much you know now that you did not know before? You've learned everything from how to greet and how to express your emotions to basics like colors and place words. You can tell time and ask question. All without opening a schoolbook. Instead, you've cruised through fun, interesting stories and possibly listened to them as well.

Perhaps before you weren't able to distinguish meaning when you listened to Spanish. If you used the audiobook, we bet you can now pick out meanings and words when you hear someone speaking. Regardless, we are sure you have taken an important step to being more fluent. You are well on your way!

Best of all, you have made the essential step of distinguishing in your mind the idea that most often hinders people studying a new language. By approaching Spanish through our short stories and dialogs, instead of formal lessons with just grammar and vocabulary, you are no longer in the 'learning' mindset. Your approach is much more similar to an osmosis, focused on speaking and using the language, which is the end goal, after all!

So, what's next?

This is just the first of five books, all packed full of short stories and dialogs, covering essential, everyday Spanish that will ensure you master the basics. You can find the rest of the books in the series, as well as a whole host of other resources, at LearnLikeNatives.com. Simply add the book to your library to take the next step in your language learning journey. If you are ever in need of new ideas or direction, refer to our 'Speak Like a Native' eBook, available to you for free at LearnLikeNatives.com, which clearly outlines practical steps you can take to continue learning any language you choose.

We also encourage you to get out into the real world and practice your Spanish. You have a leg up on most beginners, after all—instead of pure textbook learning, you have been absorbing the sound and soul of the language. Do not underestimate the foundation you have built reviewing the chapters of this book. Remember, no one feels 100% confident when they speak with a native speaker in another language.

One of the coolest things about being human is connecting with others. Communicating with someone in their own language is a wonderful gift. Knowing the language turns you into a local and opens up your world. You will see the reward of learning languages for many years to come, so keep that practice up!. Don't let your fears stop you from taking the chance to use your Spanish. Just give it a try, and remember that you will make mistakes. However, these mistakes will teach you so much, so view every single one as a small victory! Learning is growth.

Don't let the quest for learning end here! There is so much you can do to continue the learning process in an organic way, like you did with this book. Add another book from Learn Like a Native to your library. Listen to Spanish talk radio. Watch some of the great Spanish films. Put on the latest

CD from Rosalia. Take salsa lessons in Spanish. Whatever you do, don't stop because every little

step you take counts towards learning a new language, culture, and way of communicating.

www.LearnLikeNatives.com

Learn Like a Native is a revolutionary **language education brand** that is taking the linguistic world by storm. Forget boring grammar books that never get you anywhere, Learn Like a Native teaches you languages in a fast and fun way that actually works!

As an international, multichannel, language learning platform, we provide **books, audio guides and eBooks** so that you can acquire the knowledge you need, swiftly and easily.

Our **subject-based learning**, structured around real-world scenarios, builds your conversational muscle and ensures you learn the content most relevant to your requirements. Discover our tools at ***LearnLikeNatives.com***.

When it comes to learning languages, we've got you covered!

CPSIA information can be obtained
at www.ICGtesting.com
Printed in the USA
BVHW040606011220
594592BV00002B/23